Trading Cryptocurrencies: A Beginner's Guide

Bitcoin, Ethereum, Litecoin

Clem Chambers

ADVFN BOOKS

Contents

Introduction

This is a short book because time is no one's friend in the market. As I write, Bitcoin and a wave of other cryptocoins (called altcoins) are going wild. This is the dotcom bubble all over again, and if you can trade it and not blow up your account you can make a killing.

But cryptocurrencies are not shares, nor bonds, options or commodities. Bitcoins and all the other cryptocurrencies are their own ecosystem and obey new rules that no one fully understands.

This is where risk = reward. There is big risk and the chance of big reward.

But where do you start and then what do you do?

This book will tell you and hand you ways to make money.

Chapter 1: Golden Rules

Firstly, here are a few golden rules of trading and investing, whatever you are investing in. They are anchors to hold onto in this rollercoaster ride.

Rule 1: Any fool can make money buying in a bull market.
Rule 2: All you have to know is which way the market is going.
Rule 3: Don't confuse your brains with a bull market. See rule 1.
Rule 4: Trees don't grow to the sky. Things don't go up forever.
Rule 5: Up like a rocket, down like a rock.
Rule 6: Risk = reward.

You probably want to ignore all this now because you want to get trading or investing. Once you have, you should refer back to these rules because this market is going to be like the dotcom bubble. A lot of people made a lot of money but most lost it all again. If they had known these rules and had kept to them they would have made a fat profit and not been flattened by the crash.

But let's go… it's time to get started.

Chapter 2: Getting Started

Cryptocurrency has its own trading infrastructure. Trading and investing in a cryptocurrency is quite like stocks but without many of the costs and without some of the layers.

The gold standard cryptocoin in the arena is Bitcoin. This was the first cryptocurrency, outlined by the still anonymous Satashi Nakamoto. It put together a number of ideas and consolidated them into what Bitcoin became.

Bitcoin is a distributed system, using a trustless ledger (called the blockchain) producing virtual tokens that can be a store of value and used like money. 'Trustless' means that no central issuing authority is needed, because an immutable record is kept on machines spread around the internet that act together through a machine-intermediated political process. Anyone can participate at any level without permission. The system and its use is protected, secured and driven by cryptographic processes which enable Bitcoin to be outside of centralised control, while being tamper-proof and universally accessible.

I could go on… but you get the picture. Bitcoin is cool and has lots of utility, which makes it valuable.

Bitcoin is the king of crypto and the most expensive coin.

To get going you first need to get some Bitcoins. To do that you need to exchange some 'fiat currency' for Bitcoins.

Note: Fiat currency

Fiat currency is any currency issued by a government. It can be dollars, yen, euros, pounds, reals, Aussie dollars, bhat... it's a long list but if a country issues money, it is 'fiat.'

The word fiat is a bit of a sneering term used by cryptocurrency folks to deride mainstream currencies they see as a tool for repression. Fiat means made so by decree. Fiat means "because I say so," implying it's a bit of a con trick. Fiat promises only to replace a dollar with another paper dollar, whereas once it could be swapped with gold. This classic government financial betrayal is a driver for many who love Bitcoin. Their anti-establishment viewpoint prefers money outside of governments' historical profligate control.

Anyway, it's a convenient term to bundle up all the money from the old system and not have to list individual currencies when we refer to using classic money in our trading process.

Bitcoin Exchanges

So the first job is to get some 'fiat' into Bitcoin. You need a Bitcoin exchange to send your money to.

There are a host of services for cryptocurrency. I wouldn't trust most of them more than I could throw them. The whole situation is the Wild West. So I'm not going to profile all the different players because I can't test them all. Instead, I will simply highlight the companies that I have used successfully and I feel offer a good service. This is a bootstrap for you to get going.

Coinbase.com

This is the main exchange I use. It is an American company, and it is the big name in this game. It accepts wire transfers and it takes credit cards.

Credit cards are a fast way of getting funds in play, if you are not a fan of messing around with bank transfers and holding on the line with your bank waiting for permission to send your own money. In the end, however, if you want to move significant sums only a wire will do, but to get started and get a taste, a few hundred from a credit card is a fast way to get some coin to play with.

There are many other exchanges that are like Coinbase, for example, Kraken. But I have settled on Coinbase.

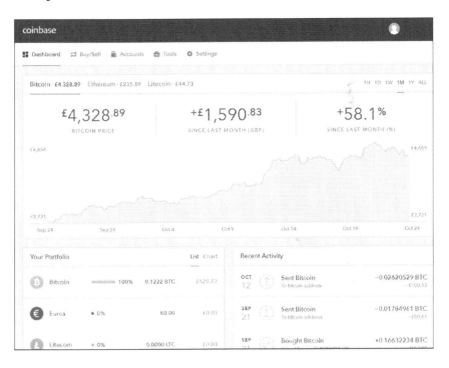

It is sensible to go with the one, master account you can trust and then move coins to other venues from there. It is a realistic possibility that any such venue can be robbed. Many exchanges have been robbed, have disappeared, or have been busted or shuttered by the authorities, so going with the gold standard is the best strategy to have at the moment.

> **Note: Be Sceptical**
>
> We are not in Kansas now. The cryptocurrency world is awash with scammers. At every turn someone is trying to rob or rip you off. To avoid this, you must have all your wits about you. Do not do anything you are not 100% sure about and even then be very sceptical. For instance, believe what I write here but do not trust it. Check out the publisher of this book, read up about me. Make sure I'm not a scammer luring you into a scheme. Now repeat this for everything you do in this sphere. Knowledge is the way to make money here. Finding things in this space you can trust and understand is most of the way to making good profits. If you are going to take big risks, control everything you can around that to avoid unfortunate outcomes. It is the same with stocks but this is way more sketchy.

It takes time to open accounts with the exchanges that take fiat funds. This can be intimidating and a bit scary. You will have to go through a fairly detailed account-opening process. They put you through a lot of KYC (know your customer) checks.

Coinbase do solid checks, which I like for a repository of my funds. They also limit the size of transactions you can do at first, to protect themselves and the new user.

The KYC information is a lot of sensitive data, which is another reason to keep a narrow focus with the exchanges you use and to use only the most reputable.

I use Coinbase as the equivalent of a master account. Fiat goes in and cryptocurrency goes out. Likewise I put cryptocurrency in and send fiat back to my classic banking accounts. I have sent funds in and out this way without a hitch.

I test everything with all providers with small amounts. It doesn't always work with all services out there. I have had money from exchanges not show up at my bank; as such they don't get to serve me. You should do likewise, just to get comfortable with the system and your provider.

Going through this test loop takes time and costs money, but it could turn out much more expensive if you don't. To get going now, opening an account with Coinbase is the way to go.

More about Coinbase

Coinbase only lets you buy and sell three coins: Bitcoin, Ethereum and Litecoin.

Some exchanges offer hundreds of different coins but most will not take fiat deposits. With those exchanges you deposit Bitcoin rather than fiat. While Coinbase only offers these three coins, they are three of the biggest available.

Coinbase is best thought of as a fiat exchange and investment platform for Bitcoin, Ethereum and Litecoin, which can be a repository from which to send Bitcoin to other venues for trading.

Coinbase doesn't have trading facilities of the sophistication, breath and complexity of other exchanges. It doesn't set out to be a trading venue, it is a portal between classical banking and the new financial world of cryptocurrencies. This might seem a weakness, but it is actually a strength. There is far too much complexity elsewhere. Keeping the entry and exit point for your funds simple and user friendly is a definite benefit.

I consider Coinbase a kind of vault.

Note: Security

Security is heavy in cryptocurrency. In some ways cryptocurrency websites go to greater lengths to secure themselves than online banks. It's a good job too as there is an army of hackers trying to steal your coins. There are many ways to secure your coins but the main two are: hold them on an online service like Coinbase or hold them on a computer or other device in a so-called 'wallet.'

You can download cryptocurrency wallets onto your computer or mobile and they hold the keys to your coins. These keys allow you to move the coins, transact with them and check how many you have or if you have received any.

Lose the wallet and your coins are gone. You can secure the wallet in a series of complicated fallbacks, like master passwords, but the basic weakness of holding your coins on your computer or even as printouts is that you can lose them forever, just like keeping gold in a safe in your basement. Literally billions of dollars of Bitcoins have been lost this way. If you hold them on an online exchange, you can still lose the lot if the exchange is lost, or you lose the passwords. Security is a minefield and the best defence is to spread your coins around.

In my opinion and as someone who loses phones regularly, it's best to keep your coins on exchanges.

Trading Sites

So you buy Bitcoin and then send them to your trading venues. These trading venues are also exchanges but they have a spread of coins you can trade.

There are now thousands of different coins to play with. Exchange trading venues are like stock markets, so this is where the trading occurs.

Like stocks, all coins are not equal. There are crypto-Googles and there are crazy Pink Sheet stock-like cryptocoins.

These 'not-Bitcoins' are called ALTCOINS.

Some altcoins, like Ethereum, are made by brilliant teams of well-funded developers; some are made by kids in high school. Some are worth hundreds of dollars each and have billion dollar market caps, while others are worth fractions of a cent with a market cap of a few thousand dollars. Some have purpose beyond being a coin, some are copies of other coins with no purpose but to be gambled with on an exchange.

Some coins have been launched and disappeared again. Some coins are broken or neglected. New ones appear every day. There are few rules, so you can buy a coin and it can simply vanish or just become worthless, but it might quintuple.

It's a dazzling, confusing, crazy buffet of pure trading risk.

Because the full spectrum of coins is so broad, many exchanges concentrate on a subset of coins; these exchanges operate in a kind of hierarchy, just like the stock markets of the USA, where you have:

- NYSE – traditional home for the big blue chips of the US economy.
- NASDAQ – home for racy tech stocks, many never as safe as the giant old economy stocks of the NYSE.
- OTCBB – risky stocks with little regulation.
- Pink Sheets – crazy stocks for wild trading. Pure gambling stocks in a market rife with upset.
- Grey sheets – do these companies even exist?

This model works well in cryptocurrency. You have the big three, the blue chip coins, on Coinbase: Bitcoin, Ethereum and Litecoin. Then you go to other exchange to trade the rest.

Here are the exchanges I use.

Bittrex.com

This is an excellent site to trade all the top tier coins and a few of the more crazy ones. When Bitcoin split into two coins in July 2017, the original Bitcoin and the new Bitcoin cash, Bittrex was one of the few exchanges that gave the new coin to Bitcoin-holders immediately. I made $900 a coin while others were forced to watch as they did not receive their coins and many never will.

So Bittrex is my main trading venue and holds a stash of coins in my wallets there. They will also take mining deposits. Other exchanges won't, so this is a definite plus. (More about mining in a later chapter.)

But Bittrex doesn't handle all the altcoins that exist, so you need more exchanges. This is not just to trade more coins, it is to let you do trading between exchanges as well, which is an opportunity to make money. (I explain this later.)

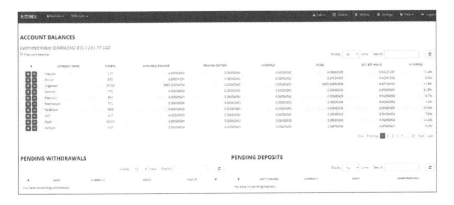

Coinexchange.io

This site trades more of the small cap coins. I want to call them crazy coins but frankly you have to embrace the madness to make money. You have to understand its extreme risk, which is why you can make good money. If you pare away the risk by analysing the coins you want to trade, you get to the good opportunities amongst the chaos. The smaller the coins the greater the opportunity.

Novaexchange.com

Note: Novaexchange closing

Within a couple of weeks of writing the first draft of this book, Novaexchange announced they were shutting down. On the surface it is because they are selling to new owners who want to use the exchange software with a clean start. As such, son of Novaexchange may rise from the ashes. Novaexchange is still running as I write but is closing down in phases. This is a perfect example of how this market place is developing. It is basically mad. I could have deleted this part but it plays a role in showing how quickly developing and sketchy the whole arena is. By the time you read this they will likely be gone and its predecessor be up and running... Or not. What this means is you cannot sit back for long; you have to be vigilant and be ready to head for the exit in any coin, token or facilitator.

Novaexchange has yet more coins you have never heard of. This is where you go to look for the next Bitcoin. A coin you can buy a million of for $30 on the dream it will rise massively like Bitcoin or Ethereum and be worth $1m in five years. Meanwhile, it could also quadruple in the next month. This is the game of investing in altcoins, it's a 'Hollywood or bust' trade.

Cryptopia.co.nz

Yet again here there are more coins to trade and arbitrage. The more exchanges you have access to, the more opportunities present themselves. However, there is only so much complexity you can handle. As such I have kept to these exchanges plus one more...

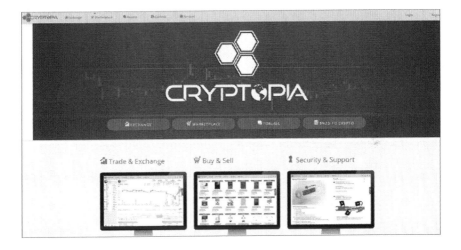

Yobit.net

At the mad end of altcoin is Yobit. There are coins on Yobit that don't even exist anymore except in theory. This is the wildest end of the Wild West that is cryptocoin trading.

The site will even give you free coins, even the odd fragment of a Bitcoin now and again. This is the seething basement of cryptocurrency. You wouldn't want to leave a lot of Bitcoin sploshing around here but the site works, you can transfer Bitcoin in and out again. In this casino, when you win you take your money off the table and leave. This isn't to decry this site – it is great, but you can never be too careful with any player in this market. The bigger they are, the bigger a target they are for criminals; the smaller they are, the more likely they are to be fragile. As long as you are careful, you will be OK, but you need to keep your level of paranoia high.

With Coinexchange, Bittrex and other exchanges, price differences occur that can give you arbitrage opportunities. More on that later.

TradeSatoshi

The Cryptocurrency market moves at lightning speed. Since starting to write the book a few weeks ago, coins and exchanges have come and gone. My favourite mad microcap coin is BOAT. It has had its wallet implode on Coinexchange.io, who knows why, and Novaexchange has announced it is closing down. That is two of this coin's major exchanges in conniptions. This has led me to TradeSatoshi, yet another exchange that lists crazy coins. It has a nice front end and is easy to use and fast to join. This is where I'll be doing BOAT trading unless Coinexchange.io gets its wallet fixed. (Stop press – just before going to press, I see that Coinexchange has fixed the BOAT wallet!) This is why rewards can be so great, because the risks are so varied and unpredictable and who knows, BOAT could pop up on other exchanges and all kinds of unexpected madness could happen. Meanwhile TradeSatoshi.com goes in the book.

Summary

To summarise, here are the steps you need to go through to get going:

1. Open a Coinbase account. Be prepared for a lot of KYC.
2. Fund it with some money. Credit card funding is immediate.
3. Put that money into Bitcoin. Start at the top of the food chain.
4. Open accounts with the following exchanges:
   - Bittrex
   - Coinexchange.io
   - Crytopia
   - Yobit
   - TradeSatoshi

When you want to trade, send Bitcoin from Coinbase to these exchanges and buy and trade altcoins in and out of Bitcoin.

You are now in the game.

If you want to turn your coins into fiat, send Bitcoin back to Coinbase and cash out from there.

We will address how to actually play the game in later chapters.

Chapter 3: Investing in Cryptocurrency

There are many investment styles that are ways to invest in things, be that art, stocks or property. These tried and tested techniques can be applied to cryptocoins. Here are some of the permutations:

1. *Buy the best and hold them, stock market style*
   On the first of the month, take what you are comfortable with investing in blue chip coins like Bitcoin then convert some of your fiat into that coin. Choose at random between Bitcoin, Ethereum or Litecoin and try to keep roughly the same amount in fiat terms of each. Every year decide if you want to add another blue chip cryptocoin to your portfolio to broaden it, but probably stick to those three. Watch the portfolio grow while forgetting what it is worth in fiat. In 20 years it should be worth a decent pile of fiat money. This is what the precious metal hoarders call stacking but it is just saving money in something that is not fiat cash.

2. *Buy a broad based portfolio of cryptocurrency*
   With a growing experience in what you can expect to get from cryptocurrency, you pick coins you believe have a good future and buy chunks of new coins until you have 30+ different coins in your cryptocurrency portfolio. You look out for opportunities, evaluate the fundamentals of coins and make your investments accordingly. You hold until you think a particular coin has risen enough or is broken and likely to become worthless, sell it and move into other coins. This is like classic stock picking with equities. It's more work/fun and should give higher returns.

3. *Buy and hold, high-risk cryptocurrency style*
   Find new coins with very low prices because they are new. Buy a

lot of coins for little fiat then forget them for many years on the basis that one will go big but others will likely vanish. This is attempting to reproduce the story of Bitcoin. If you had bought $10 worth of Bitcoin at the beginning it would now be worth $3m. In 2010, 10,000 Bitcoins ($35 million at today's prices) were used to buy two pizzas. This is the logic behind this trade. For $1,000 you could buy 100 such lottery tickets and if one pays off you will be very happy indeed. With cryptocoins having a global total value of $135 billion as I type this, it could happen. There are roughly $47 trillion dollars of US equities and US government bonds out there; it is not unimaginable that cryptocurrency could match gold at a total value of $5 trillion. That is room for a lot of Bitcoin stories.

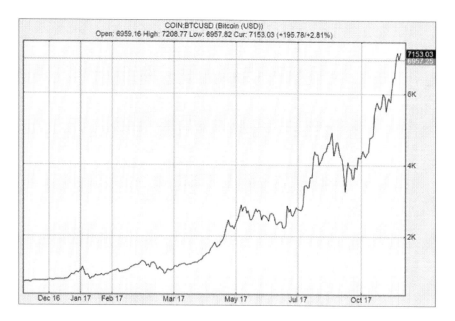

So the question is: how high could Bitcoin go?

This is an interesting question because the value of Bitcoin rains down on all the altcoins below.

You can come up with your own theories because no one knows. Here are some of mine.

1. The first idea is obvious. Bitcoin could go to $0. It's just a hula-hoop. It will be banned. It will be cracked. It's just madness. This could happen, but let's go back to Golden Rule 2: we are sure this is not going to happen.

2. Cryptocurrency is the new gold. There is $5 trillion of gold in the world. Why not $5 trillion of Bitcoin and altcoins? That's about $100,000 a Bitcoin.

3. There is $13 trillion of US money, but $19 trillion in US government debt. That's a gap of $6 trillion dollars – not enough US cash to cover the US government's debt. That is creating a monetary vacuum that Bitcoin will fill, and would need one Bitcoin to be worth half a million bucks at the current level of issuance. (There is also $25 trillion in shares needing money to transact, so this idea has a certain attraction for me.)

4. Cryptocurrency could be as big as the NYSE stock market, which has a current total market cap of $17 trillion. That's equivalent to well over a million dollars per Bitcoin.

5. Bitcoins have 100,000,000 fractions, called satoshis. If each fraction was worth a US cent, the biggest convenient fragment, then a Bitcoin would be worth $1,000,000. I like this one especially because it is so simple, contains lots of zeros, is hilariously huge, just looks good on paper and is crazy enough to be right. (But don't bank on it)

Surely this is madness – let's go back to Golden Rule 4. Trees don't grow to the sky. Things don't go up forever.

But we should think again. We must try and forget what we think we know, we must keep our minds as open as possible and even stretch them.

So let us do a little mental work out.

The maximum number of Bitcoins is 21 million (that's the hard limit that the creators put in place), so at $1,000,000 each that would be $21 trillion dollars of Bitcoin.

Impossible?

Yes!

Really?

Well…

…

…

…

…

…

…

…

…

No…

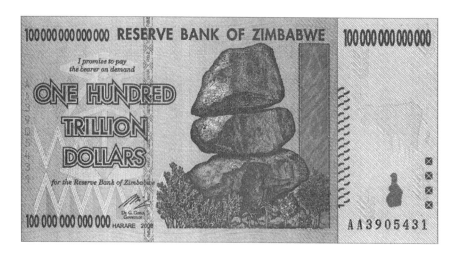

…not impossible, just inconceivable.

To be fair, no one knows.

There is a shortage of money in the world and that is helping to drive cryptocurrency prices.

Then there is the fact I can send money to someone on the other side of the world in a few minutes with Bitcoin, Litecoin etc. I simply cannot do that with fiat. I can hang on the phone for ages waiting for a poor barely coherent call centre person to sort me out. I might be asked why I'm sending it and where I got it from. It might take two or three days to arrive. Heaven forbid I wanted to send it to somewhere difficult like most of South America, Asia or Eastern Europe.

Bitcoin or Litecoin does the job in minutes, even seconds.

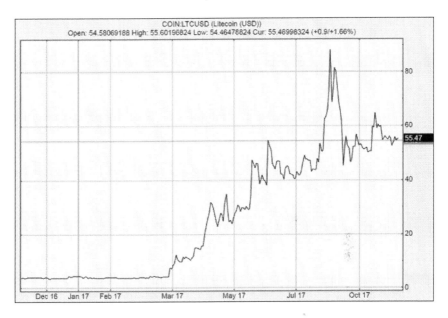

Try opening a bank account in the modern age! Getting an altcoin wallet takes no time at all. I can get it, install it, get coin and send it on in the time it takes to hold for the next available operator to answer my query and tell me to post my electricity bill to them.

There is one more thing powering cryptocurrency: an actual shortage of cash in the global system.

The state of M2 (cash and near cash) in the US economy is a very interesting situation. The US has $19 trillion in debt and $13 trillion in money and another $50 trillion in assets like stocks, corporate bonds etc. $13 trillion in money doesn't strike me as enough to make the US economy system spin fluidly. Economists grumble that there is no inflation and no growth and it seems to me that both would be caused by too little money.

Economics will always find a way and perhaps it is cryptocurrency that is filling the need for more money, and satisfying that old fashioned need to have enough medium of exchange in circulation, to meet demand.

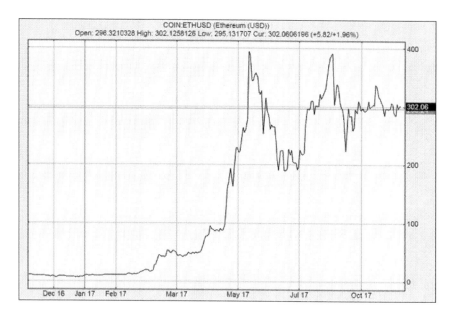

So how high can Bitcoin go?

I personally think $100,000 is a good long-term target, with the other coins adding the other trillion(s) of dollars needed to the money pool.

Many governments will fight it but then they will realise that this money is real wealth and to block it is to turn away money. A lot of money is created in the private sector by banks. Cryptocurrency being created in the private sector is not much different.

Cryptocurrency creation is a tap of wealth that can flow a new kind of wealth into economies. This can be taxed like any other asset… and it will be.

If cryptocurrency can rise to that kind of valuation, the question of when is another question entirely. Surely it will take years, but in reality no one knows.

Initial Coin Offerings

An Initial Coin Offering (ICO) is a fundraising mechanism in which new projects sell their underlying crypto tokens in exchange for Bitcoin or other altcoins. They are like a Kickstarter for coin start-ups.

Right now ICOs are hot. As I write over $2 billion dollars has been raised via ICO, and a whirlwind of interest is to be followed by a whirlwind of regulation.

Do not be deceived; most ICOs will not deliver on their promises. Many are straight out frauds. This might sound dire and it is, but the same might be said about stock IPOs. Stocks on the stock markets are riddled with scandal and fraud and dubious practices that never come to light. If you don't believe me, just surf the financial pages for a few months to see a procession of them. However, ICOs are an amplification of this.

That is not to say some won't turn into massive businesses or blockchain phenomena. Anyone looking at an ICO with a view to invest must understand they will lose all their investment in nine out of ten and that they are looking for the tiny minority of them that will go up fifty times in the next decade. This makes investing in ICOs not for the faint-hearted.

From a stock market point of view, most ICOs are a joke. Anyone trying it on in this sort of way with a listed company would be thrown off the market and probably into jail.

However risk = reward. It is the rare ICO that comes good that delivers the reward.

There are a couple of ways to proceed if you want to play this dangerous game.

1. Research an ICO to death. Avoid anything that isn't at the tip-top of quality. Ignore anything at all sketchy. Then keep digging until you are 200% sure you aren't dealing with a pile of flim-flam. If you have even a tiny scintilla of doubt avoid it. Expect to hit one success in four and invest accordingly.

2. Research an ICO to death but buy a little of each that passes your acid tests. Expect to hit one success in ten and invest accordingly.

Some ICOs are just an opportunity to buy coins in a new currency. This is a simple and pure play. Do you think the coin will succeed? Do you think the folks behind it are honest and ethical? If so you can take a gamble. If not, why would you? Don't make the mistake of falling for FOMO (fear of missing out) as it is much better to miss out than lose your money. Opportunities come and go, money not so much.

The more complicated ones promise to give you something more than a coin. For example, they can be like a share or a bond and pay out the owners based on future performance. These coins are problematic as the rules on them are changing fast. A few months ago, these coins/tokens were outside of the law but now they are quickly being embraced by global financial regulators. If they promise something in the future like a dividend or a profit share, then they might be considered securities, like shares and bonds, and if they are issued to the wrong people in the wrong place bad things could happen. These things would probably mean the organisation behind them will fail. If you are an American and don't have a million bucks or two you will be disqualified from holding them.

However, this is a fast-changing environment. Proper companies are bound to do ICOs soon and they will be regulated and legitimate, so the best thing to do is to skill up on them and dip your toe in with money you can afford to lose. Development will deliver good profitable opportunities; you should be ready by getting on the ball now.

Chapter 4: Trading Cryptocurrency

Trading is not investing. Trading is making short-term money from short-term positions based on the movement of prices driven by technical matters.

For example, most people buy and sell shares or forex or Bitcoin on news. The trader takes a position based on their gauge of how long the market is taking to reprice the instrument and holds their position until they feel that price level is reached.

Trading should not be a guessing game and if it is, it becomes costly.

The Trading Tools

The key trading tool is an order management platform. In a primitive system you enter your order and it gets filled.

But trading is an arms race, so it is no good simply having a system like this because others will have a more complex and sophisticated one that gives them execution advantage and thereby they can run rings around you, lowering your profitability. For example, they will get to the trade first and more accurately than you and you will be left flat with the crumbs of the action.

Luckily most exchanges have sophisticated tools, at least as clever and often more leading edge than mammoth equity brokerages offer their customers.

Brokerages charge a lot of money for tools like real time prices and order book access. These tools are generally only used by the pros in stock market trading, but in cryptocurrency these tool types are broadly available to everyone.

The key to trading in most financial instruments is a Level 2 order book. This shows all the orders to passively buy and sell and lets you enter yours anywhere.

This is a key to profits in trading as you can, for example, put in your order so that it is only executed if someone wants to give you a better-than-current price and you are prepared to wait. If you order classically, someone offers a price and you take it. You are a price taker. The person offering a price is a price maker and is usually a market professional or institution. Price makers have an advantage which is one of the reasons you don't get that tool unless you spend or trade a lot.

When you trade cryptocurrencies, the uneven playing field of equities is easy to see. The layers of middlemen clipping you as you go are suddenly lit in high relief.

But we aren't playing the equity game; with cryptocurrency we have all the tools and much lower costs, so let's get to it.

What follows are some simple ways to make money using a cryptocurrency exchange's Level 2.

Market Making

Market makers are the Ali Babas of the stock market. They skim the market and provide liquidity. Exchanges and regulators give them special rules to let them skim the market because they are scared that without them the stock markets won't work. Or maybe it is because stock markets are a kind of cosy club...

Anyway, there aren't any regulators or special rules for market making on cryptocoins. You can be a market maker yourself.

Market makers set the price they want to get if they sell something, called the Ask (or in the UK the Offer) and the price they will pay to buy something, the Bid. Then they wait for someone to accept those prices. They set the Ask higher than the Bid and make money on the difference between them – known as capturing the spread. This can be very little or it can be a massive percentage. If you can buy on the Bid and sell on the Ask every time, and quickly, you would make giant sums. Market makers in stocks do just that, but you can imagine that at that scale it is a more complex business than I am about to demonstrate.

Let's take my favourite minnow coin, Doubloon (its ticker symbol is BOAT) as an example.

Its Bid/Ask is a huge 100/115. If you want to buy now, you have to pay 115, if you want to sell you can get 100. That's a 15% difference. That means, if you bought 10,000 Doubloons and sold them again, you would lose 15% of your money. The person offering to buy and sell would make 15%.

So you can see the opportunity and the danger here.

Now forgetting the poor buyer, you could be offering to buy at 101, rather than hit the 115 Ask, and offer to sell at 114 rather than dump at 100, and you would be at the head of these order queues. If a person sold to you for 101 and another bought off you for 114, you have just made a very fat profit.

How do you get those offers onto the order book?

Simple: you just make your order at that price and it will sit there until it's filled. There is no guarantee anyone will contract at that price and someone may jump ahead of you to offer to buy at a better 102 or sell at 113. This is how spreads come in and become small in bigger coins.

However, you are free to leapfrog them too. That is how the spread gets to be perhaps 106/107.

That is how market making and markets work, except in established markets professional companies have carved out this niche and protect it from outsiders *(for your own good, of course).*

Yes, many coins have fat spreads and you can put orders on both sides, or on one side at a time, and attempt to capture the value of that spread. I've done it on occasion and I reckon it could pay a full time wage for those who fancy sitting at the screen all day making markets.

Happily, the days that I would want to spend my time doing that are long past, but for others less fortunate or less busy, it makes perfect sense to make a living that way.

Clearly things can go wrong. For example, you sell at 115 and fail to buy back at 100 and the price roars to 200. You won't get your coins back at 100. However, over time, if you are always on or near the Bid and Ask with orders, on average you will get the spread.

This is why banks, brokers and market makers need capital, because they make money on average and have to have money behind them to take losses until the profits roll in. If you bought some coins and the market immediately crashed you'd end up with nothing left to trade with.

The beauty is, you can test the method out yourself with $10 of a small cryptocoin, market making with satoshi-sized amounts. Just pick a coin with a decent spread and off you go. If you tried it in stocks you'd need at least tens of thousands and perhaps hundreds of thousands of dollars to even play around a little.

So this is not one of those ideas you need a huge pile of cash to try. You can jump on any exchange, pop in 0.01 BTC and use that to tinker with this idea for days.

This is one of the refreshing beauties of cryptocurrencies. The negligible costs and the lack of the onerous burden of regulation make it a playground for those who want to skill up. The downside is that the arena is rife with predators. That risk is real but balancing that, the opportunity more than compensates if you have your wits about you.

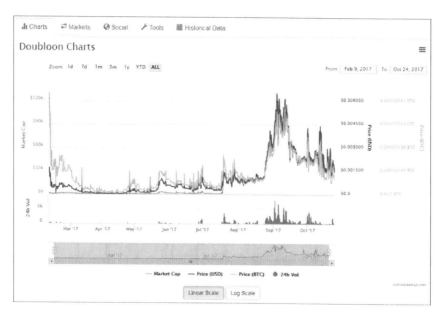

Trading Different Coins

Investing and trading are two different things entirely. An investor in cryptocurrencies is best off buying a bunch of different ones and forgetting about them for three years, hoping one will go to the moon. A trader wants a short-term profit.

However, it is hard to keep track of dozens of coins if you are looking for a short-term rise.

Since I've been playing these coins I have decided I prefer to sell them when they rally 3-400%. That is an insane return in the short term and I don't really want to miss that for the prospect of a 1,000% in many years' time.

This is how I keep track of it: I will buy, for example 0.3 of a Bitcoin; it might as well be 0.03 or 0.003, the principle is the same. When I am checking my positions I look for a coin that is now worth more than 1 Bitcoin and if it is, I simply sell it without thinking.

These events don't last long – perhaps only an hour or two. I have missed some because I've been away from my desk or travelling. This method works because the market is so explosive and frothy. In shares you would do this for 30%, watching over months as the classic value investors used to do, but this is a 'fast' market in a boom and fast times require fast reactions.

Please remember this is not how normal markets work, this is a once-in-a-generation event where timescales are telescoped. As a novice or even a seasoned investor you need to keep your position sizes small and realise trading cryptocurrency is walking a tightrope without a net.

If you set out to add some extra returns to your overall portfolio by putting a small amount of money to work you will be left in profit cursing your lack of courage. If you show much courage you will lose a lot of money and curse your recklessness. It is better therefore to show caution and make a tidy sum rather than trash your capital when the market turns against you, as it surely will.

Punters gamble, bookmakers bet. Be a bookmaker and place clever stakes.

Trading On Other Exchanges

Sometimes the same coin can be listed at different prices on different exchanges. This gives you an opportunity to make money. Taking Doubloons (BOAT) as an example, it is listed on Novaexchange and Coinexchange and you can see that prices are different on both.

People simply can't be bothered to chop and change so one exchange has most of the traffic, in this case as I write it's Coinexchange. Because of that the prices are different:

Coinexchange price is 119/120

Novaexchange is 100/117

As I'm writing this I have just bought 800 Doubloons at 117 on Novaexchange and sold 800 at 119 on Coinexchange. OK, that's only 7c in profit but I was only looking for an example of this kind of price opportunity and to actually execute the trade, so it wasn't just a theoretical exercise.

Keeping things real is important to me and I consider it imperative not to be in the crowd of boosters that lure the unwary into activities on the basis of lies.

I could quite easily have executed this trade with 20,000 Doubloons and therefore made nearly $2 in two minutes. Many would like to be paid $2 a minute.

To do this you must have Bitcoin on both exchanges and a balance of the coins you want to market make, on both sites. If you get low on Bitcoin or the coin you are trading on one site, you should have naturally built it up on the other side by the process of buying and selling. As such, every now and again if the balance goes to one exchange, you send Bitcoin or the coin you are trading between exchanges to keep balances sufficient to stay ready and loaded.

This is where capital comes in. The more Bitcoin you have, the more coins you can trade between exchanges.

So I bought $4 of Doubloons and sold $4 on another exchange and made 7c. That might not be big money but when scaled it is a business model. It is called arbitrage and Wall Street is based on it.

So we can market make and arbitrage, that is two ways to coin coins, and by doing so you help the markets keep their prices sensible and give other traders the ability to buy and sell at better prices than if you weren't there.

It's a win-win.

To make this really work all you have to do is follow multiple coins on multiple exchanges looking for the opportunities. You then have to move as fast as possible to capture the differences. You also need to become accustomed to the various exchanges and what they have to offer.

As always, it's a skill game and the more practice you get and the more skill you develop, the more you will make.

Summary

So to recap: You can sit on the Bid and Ask of a cryptocurrency to capture the spread. This can be a huge percentage on some coins. Some coins will have a minimal spread, while others will have a fat one. Some days the spreads will be bigger than others. The faster the market is moving the bigger the spreads will be and you will make the most money when the market is at its riskiest.

You can trade between different coins, taking advantage of the price fluctuations.

You can arbitrage between exchanges, buying where it is cheaper on the Ask and then selling on the Bid on another site where the Bid is higher than the Ask on the site you bought on.

With so many new coins coming on the market and all of them valued in Bitcoin there will continue to be these mispricings and it is the job of the trader to trade them away. This is what a trader gets paid to do, make the market efficient by playing on inefficiencies and errors.

It will pay you too, if you have the time and patience.

Chapter 5: Advanced Investing

Investing in cryptocurrency seems pretty mad. The market is mad. The volatility is mad. The idea is mad to many. There aren't any rules, just theses to be tested in a Wild West environment.

So how can you invest?

Back to Rule 2: all you have to know is which way the market is going. So what do you say? If it is going down or you don't know, don't play. If you say up, then that is the starting point.

Selecting a Good Coin:
Some Fundamentals

So now we have to decide what makes for a good coin. That means searching the internet for the relevant data and making a judgement on what to buy.

So what makes for a good coin?

Here are my factors, the things I look at. These are long-term fundamentals and not for trading with.

Definitions

I am about to use a lot of technobabble, so here's a quick glossary of techy terms:

Mining – using your computer to solve puzzles which verify Bitcoin/altcoin transactions, in exchange for a reward and/or the transaction fee.

Mining pool – a group of miners working collectively to solve the puzzles and sharing the reward.

Algo – short for algorithm. It's the list of rules to follow in order to solve a problem; in this case it's the instructions to solve the puzzle.

ASIC-resistant – an ASIC is a special chip designed specifically to mine Bitcoins. If a coin is ASIC-resistant it means there is little or no advantage to mining it with an ASIC.

GPU – graphics processing unit. The circuit in your computer that creates the images on the screen.

CPU – central processing unit. It's the engine of your computer.

1080ti – considered (at the time of writing) the most powerful GPU you can buy for your home computer or mining rig.

The Basic Fundamentals

1. What is the algo used for mining – ASIC resistant, GPU, CPU mineable?

2. How many satoshi (fractions of a Bitcoin) is the coin worth?

3. What is the infrastructure behind it?
   a. What exchanges support it?
   b. Mining pools.

4. What is its market cap?

5. What is the maximum number of coins that can ever be created?

6. What is its inflation rate?

7. How good are the people behind the coin?

Then decide what result you want from your investments. Do you want low risk or high risk? Mark each coin out of ten and get a total score.

Using Those Fundamentals

So let's imagine we want a long-term portfolio of blue chip coins – I hesitate to say low risk. So here are some thoughts on how to ask those questions.

1. What is the algo for mining?

Bitcoin uses the SHA256 algo, the toughest nut to crack, with Bitcoin miners using warehouses of specialist computers to do their mining. It is a so-called Proof of Work algorithm that has got so hard that ASIC miners are needed to make a profit out of doing the accounting on the blockchain. It's the gold standard of cryptocurrency. Anything that moves away from the Bitcoin standard should be marked down. The further away the lower the score. You must have Bitcoin in a long-term portfolio of cryptocurrencies.

2. How many satoshi (fractions of a Bitcoin) is the coin worth?

Bigger is better. Successful coins can be worth hundreds of dollars each, not fractions of a cent. Their ongoing success is some security for the future. This must be combined with market cap. A big coin with a low market cap would be a joke coin. So an expensive coin with a good market cap is a lower risk investment because folk already trust it and are treating it like it is an established asset worthy of being worth tens or hundreds of dollars a coin.

3. What is the infrastructure behind it?

The more infrastructure behind a coin the better. Coinbase, the big daddy of this industry, has only three coins, so those are the coins worth hoarding. The more online and offline resources for a coin the better, and those resources can be online information sites, exchanges, wallets, mining pools, mining companies… you name it. The more a coin has participants, the more likely that it will be a big winner over the coming years.

4. What is its market cap?

Big is always beautiful in times of high risk. Score accordingly.

5. What is the maximum number of coins that can ever be created?

More coins = dilution of value. The closer a coin is to its issuance limit the better. If it has no limit, what will happen to the value of a coin as the total number of coins expands forever? The answer is obvious; more supply ultimately means less value. Meanwhile, most Bitcoins are already mined: there is a limit of 21 million ever with nearly 17 million mined already. At some point no new ones with be mined. Meanwhile, some will be lost every day through lost passwords and crashed hard disks, in the same way gold is lost every day when it falls from fingers, wrists and necks. It is intuitive that this supply limit must push up the price of the currency over time while ever-increasing supply would supress value.

6. What is its inflation rate?

This is the amount by which a coin can expand its money supply every year. Demand must outstrip this to make the coin rise in price. The more inflation you have the tougher it is for the coin to rise in value.

7. How good are the people behind the coin?

A coin is only as good and honest as the people behind it. The better the community involved with the coin and the leaders of the community are, the better the likely outcome. However, perhaps even better is a situation where no one is in control and the system takes care of itself, like Bitcoin. Even then the original developer's vision, coupled with the current development community's skills and their engagement, all add to the value of the coin. Gauging this is a good guide to the future of any coin.

But you don't have to follow this template. Make your own criteria and score it your way. At least you will end up with a ranked list of coins for your thesis on this unknowable and byzantine situation.

It can be a fun process and it is necessary if you are going to outperform any random person, buying randomly.

Putting This Into Practice

Now let's take the same template and rank it for coins that might go up a zillion per cent in the next five years or crash and burn. I will use a favourite from my speculative portfolio: Doubloon, which has the ticker BOAT. I have 30-50 such coins but this is an example of why I selected this one using the criteria.

1. What is the algo for mining?

How about an algo that lets everyone grab some coins? An algo like HMQ1725.

HMQ1725 is ASIC-resistant and can be mined with CPU and GPU. Depending on the market a 1080ti will earn you $3-$6 of Doubloons because ASIC miners can't hog all the mining.

That way it will get support from lots of small miners, which can drive interest and slingshot the coin from obscurity. I have a ton of Doubloons because it was obtainable in big quantities for cheap and I can mine 300-20,000+ a day. If the coin catches the imagination, in five years it could be $1 a coin and I would make a small fortune from basically nothing. It could happen because it tightly fits my thesis. It's a 10/1 runner with a 1,000/1 payout. Any backer has to take those odds. All it will take is one of my 30 to do this and I'm a happy guy.

Score = 8

2. How many satoshi (fractions of a Bitcoin) is the coin worth?

How about tiny 0.00000025? So small everyone can imagine the profit they will make if it goes to 0.01. It's the psychology of penny stocks and even today after generations of penny stock traders have passed through this fallacy it still has massive potency. Doubloon was 28 satoshis; it is now 100, but even so it is still a small satoshi coin, like a penny stock. People love penny stocks! At 100 it is roughly 0.5c a coin. Bitcoin is $4,500 a coin.

Cryptocurrency is full of novices so this will be a powerful theme and to be frank I can feel the pleasure of buying 1,000,000 coins for $20 and dreaming of them hitting $4,000. It happened to Bitcoin. In 2010 a pizza got bought for 10,000 Bitcoins, which is currently worth $35m.

OK it won't happen but the dream is a driver of value in the ultra-speculative end. People imagine the fortunes they would make with their 10,000 coins if they were $4,500 a coin and that is a driver. Hopium and greed are powerful forces.

Score = 8

3. What is the infrastructure behind it?

The more the merrier. It has mining pools, two good exchanges and support from CCMINER, one of the leading mining tools – pretty good for a coin that had a market cap of $18,000. It's now $100,000 as I write, but has fallen back to $50,000 as I correct this piece.

If a coin can be mined but it's not easy to mine it will have less interest and that means a lower value. Any coin with a market cap of $50,000 can go to $50m or $0. Many will go to zero and not many to

$50m and beyond. One of the key points will be support from exchanges and mining pools and mining software providers. The more support, the greater the demand, the bigger the upside.

An obscure new coin with support from mining software exchanges, pools and miners won't stay obscure for long.

Score = 7

4. What is its market cap?

The smaller the better. Bitcoin was tiny once and we want to be in on the ground floor of a new wonder asset. Buying a coin with a multibillion dollar market cap may be a good low risk investment, but so is Google. In the speculative end we want to make a life-changing win at the cost of an OK family meal in a cheap restaurant. If we plan to hold for years a coin needs a long runway to rise, like an Apple or Amazon, going from $1 or $2 to near $1,000. Why else play this wild game?

The market cap of Doubloons is $100,000. With lots of nothing burger-priced coins with $2-$5m market cap the upside is big.

Score = 8

5. What is the maximum number of coins that can ever be created?

Limited is good. Imagine the coin got to be worth $100,000,000 like many others. What is that divided by the maximum coins? If there can be 100m coins that's a dollar a coin. Doubloon was 0.1c when I bought in. A ceiling on issuance is a great feature.

Doubloon has a 500,000,000 maximum, roughly 25 times Bitcoin, but that is many years from now after a lot of mining. Even so, that many shares is not a positive but 10c a coin would 'only' be a total market cap of $50m, which would put it at number 75 in the current market cap charts – hardly a stretch – and 1,000 times pricier than it is today.

Score = 3

6. What is its inflation rate?

Low inflation is always good unless this growth rate is matched with a demand driver linked to that inflation rate. Bitcoin is tough when it comes to inflation; to make new coins takes a lot of effort and money and that effort underpins its value.

Doubloon has 50m coins a year, which is absorbable.

Score = 4

7. How good are the people behind the coin?

Great nerds make great coins. Who is behind this new baby coin? Is it a nerd or a joker? A strong development community makes a vibrant coin and a strengthening price.

It's a clean website. The coin has resources. The developer has another coin which has done well.

Score = 6

Score 44 out of 50... very good... or perhaps I'm overrating it, which is quite possible. In any event it's the process that's important. This works for cryptocoins and it works for stocks. You pick your criteria, then score the financial instruments you are researching by those criteria and then you have a ranking to make a final selection from.

Staking and Masternodes

Staking

One of the ways of making money investing in cryptocoins is called staking.

A stake is a pile of coins. If you have a stake, the system pays out a percentage of that stake to you. You get paid to hold the coins. The stake is like having a bond or a share that has a dividend attached but rather than most interest payments or dividends, you get paid daily or at least frequently.

There are coins that do this automatically by just having a wallet open with coins in it. This is another feature of my example coin, Doubloons.

Masternodes

Then there are masternodes.

Miners keep the record on the blockchain for coins. The blockchain rewards them for their work and also gives them the fees that go along with the accounting. This job is moderated by a system, which selects the bookkeeping miner for the job. The one Bitcoin uses is called Proof of Work (POW). The actual bookkeeping process doesn't take much work, but it needs to be made more difficult to slow down the rate at which new Bitcoins are created, so the POW involves solving very complicated cryptographic puzzles, with the first miner to solve a puzzle getting the reward. If you stripped this away or made it very easy then mining would be fast and easy. But then the ecosystem behind Bitcoin would likely fold because the reward enforced by the POW algo is part of the cycle that makes the whole thing tick.

However, there are different systems and one of those is Proof of Stake (POS). In this, the miner that creates the new block is chosen not by who solves the puzzle first, but by who has a stake in the coin, by having a minimum balance of coins in its attached wallet.

So you set up a masternode for a coin, for example DASH, with 1,000 coins in its wallet and it joins the masternode party receiving work and rewards for participation. For DASH this is about $52 dollars a day.

That's a nice daily payout, but wait – DASH is about $350 a coin, so $350,000 gets you, say $15,000 a year, which is about 5% per annum. That's not so hot.

However, some coins are paying 50-100% a year, but as you would imagine they are a lot more sketchy than DASH.

A good site that shows key masternode coins and their payout is: Masternodes.pro. You set up a masternode, buy enough coins to stake the masternode, and put the required coins in its wallet. Then you simply wait for the coins to roll in. The cryptocurrency system works out what you should receive and as long as the server is running you will get paid some more coins every day or so.

The king of masternodes is DASH, which started out as a system requiring $1,000 of coin to stake a masternode. Those coins are now worth $300,000+ and the daily stake interest is worth $53. A few weeks ago when the market was zooming it was paying out $223 a day.

A masternode's value is as volatile as the market for coin but as you can judge by the history of DASH, there is a lot of money to be made if you get it right.

But we mustn't let that turn our heads… too much.

The potential reward is twofold:

1. The investment in the coin pays out an income.

2. The coins can go up in value. If they do the yield goes up on your original investment and people are attracted to stake their own servers and buy the coins that will push up the price further. This is a virtuous circle.

My strategy is to buy cheap masternodes and hold them on the basis that some will prosper massively and many will die. It's the same idea as for the coins.

If you bought Apple in the early 90s or Amazon in 2001 then left them alone, you would have done very well. It's a tough strategy when you sit on a 300-400% profit because holding out for 10,000% is a feat of madness, belief and self-control few can cope with.

It is another twist on the basic idea of cryptocurrency investment.

The downside is, you need to learn how to install a masternode and this is very technical for most of us. The good news is, this skill once learned will be a massive asset to you, so it is worth doing for that alone.

Otherwise you will need to get a friendly developer to help you out.

This technical aspect is a hurdle to getting a masternode and will keep many people away, which will keep returns high. Only the top percentile of cryptocurrency traders and investors have the skill to get a masternode running and that stops the arena getting flooded by novices spoiling the opportunity.

I like masternodes because you get two bites of the cherry, the dividend and the capital upside which are lashed together by the attractiveness of the masternode model which should push both price and yield up over time if any coin masternode gets traction and takes off.

So this covers the main areas of trading and investing in cryptocurrencies. However, a little knowledge can be a dangerous thing.

There are some more golden rules of investing in general you need to embrace if you are to come out of this boom and bubble in one piece.

A vital one is diversification, which is important enough that it has a chapter of its own.

Chapter 6: Diversification

Unless you have 'Papal infallibility' (that's Papal not PayPal) you are going to be wrong a lot. You are going to be horribly wrong occasionally and you will be damn stupid sometimes too.

How can you make money as a bumbling human in this horribly complicated predator-filled jungle?

The answer is diversification. If you spread your bets you will get a good/great return on a risky market that's going up.

If you are Mr or Ms Neverwrong you can go ahead and pile into one thing with all your cash and get rich quick. Sadly, people think they are Mr Neverwrong, but they aren't and that 'all in' strategy never seems to work, or at least not for very long.

You must spread your bets.

If you want to invest in cryptocoins, then buy many. Buy 30 different ones, at least. Unlike shares, you aren't held back by fixed costs. You can buy $3 of 30 coins. You certainly can buy $33 of 30 coins and so on.

Evaluate 800 coins to get to your best 30.

You will not be affected by luck if you have 30 different coins. You won't fluke it and you won't get cursed by bad fortune. You will, however, earn your just desserts with little risk of earning less than you deserve, and that is why you must always diversify.

You don't have to be robotic about it. If you love a particular coin, you can buy two lots of it, maybe even five chunks, but don't make the mistake of putting all your money in three or four coins and hoping lightning doesn't strike you. It most likely will, at some point, and then you will get hurt badly.

The more dangerous the game – and they don't get much riskier that cryptocurrency – the more likely you are to fail in an individual investment; but to counter that, the winners are more likely to go to the moon.

That is why you have to hold many different but well-judged positions.

Take the Dotcom crash. If you had bought a random internet tech stock in 1998, a couple of years before the bubble went kaboom, you would have likely lost the lot by 2002. Even if you had bought three to four stocks, you would have probably got smashed and burnt so badly you never returned to stocks. Even if you bought Amazon you would have been bruised and bleeding by 2001-2002.

If you have bought the whole NASDAQ index at 2,000 points in 1998 via an ETF tracker fund, you would have been crowing on 31 December 1999 having turned $1 into $2.5. By 2002 that $2.5 dollars was 50c and you would have been sad but if you had just let it ride, now years later that $1 would be back over $3. OK 300% is not an amazing return in 19 years but it is better than losing the lot. The difference between losing everything and living to fight another day is the diversification you get with an index tracker that diversifies over every stock in the index.

Diversification protects the investor from what is called gambler's ruin, a state where you lose everything from 'bad luck' and can't continue to play even though overall the odds are in the player's favour.

Ultimately risk = reward, and to soften the outcome of the risk, you spread it. Diversification is a firewall for your money.

You can take a lot of losses in your investment portfolio if the survivors go on to be like Amazon or Apple. However, if you put it all in one investment and it fails, you are finished.

Novices think, "I wouldn't buy $1,000 of this coin if I thought it would become worthless." Their idea is that because they have an opinion, it will somehow guard them from error.

It will not.

It will hopefully give them an edge in being correct, but that edge is unlikely to be big enough to avoid a lot of negative outcomes. In the end there are always the 'unknown unknowns' that can spoil any investment. These unpredictable, unknowable and unavoidable futures can only be protected against by making sure that such instances won't destroy much of your capital because any one event has little impact on your financial 'big picture.' The only security for this is having a spread of risks rather than a concentration of risks.

It's extremely hard to do well in the long term if you are not diversified. It is very hard to do very well in the short term if you are diversified. However, you can bear short-term difficulties and they are overcome by time. In comparison, there is nothing sadder than someone who has lost it all from being undiversified at a point when they have no chance to repair their loss. Without diversification, catastrophic losses will punctuate an investor's history and sadly will likely end their financial story too.

If you do not diversify, then the only chance of success is to plough huge resources checking and double-checking all possible facets of your small number of investments. Even then you will be more prone to awful luck like wars, disasters, random mad politicians and other such biblical plagues. People always say they relish that work but in reality they do not do it. There will always be lottery ticket winners in the world of trading and investment and every week someone wins such a lottery, but unlike diversification you cannot bank on being lucky.

Chapter 7: Mining Cryptocoins

As I am writing this I am mining altcoins.

While my computer is running my word processor, internet connection and email, it is also mining cryptocoins.

Today my machine will make me $1.50. Tomorrow about the same. So in a year it will make me about $500 or thereabouts. That's profit after the cost of electricity.

That is the most elusive of unicorns: free money.

Free money.

I have to repeat that, because up to now there has been no such thing, at least not with computers. But here we have it, free money, $1.50 a day of it.

How do I do it?

By mining altcoins.

So what is that? What is mining?

Well, it is not mining at all, really, it's bookkeeping, but bookkeeping your computer does, not bookkeeping you have to do.

My computer is 'mining' by doing the bookkeeping for an altcoin ledger. That ledger is like Bitcoin's ledger, somewhere out on the internet on someone else's computer. This is all hooked up with other people's computers running the blockchain of the particular coin I am mining/bookkeeping.

(I won't use the term bookkeeping from here on but remember that's what mining really is.)

My computer connects to the accounting system of a coin and volunteers to do some accountancy jobs to keep track of the score as the coins on its ledger are moved about.

Now that part is simple enough but there is a nice wrinkle (by the way, in cryptocurrencies everything is full of wrinkles). This wrinkle is that you get paid in new coins to do this accountancy job, which in itself is easy, but there is a catch. To get to do the job and get the pay in new coins, you have to solve a mathematical puzzle.

This puzzle involves the computer doing some heavy number crunching. If your computer solves it, it gets the accountancy job and the reward.

That is what mining is.

So mining is like having to solve a Sudoku in the morning to be allowed to go to work. The trouble is, it can be a really tough Sudoku.

The puzzle is called a 'proof of work' algo and for a high value coin like Bitcoin it is mind-numbingly hard.

Many of these algos are so tough you have to get together in a virtual room full of other people's computers to solve the puzzle, just like most mines need many miners. These groups of miners are called a 'mining pool.' When a puzzle is solved the miners receive fair shares.

Most people mine as part of a mining pool, because going it alone means a very long wait to get anything. When the prize for solving a Bitcoin puzzle can be $60,000, with a machine that can earn just $1 a day that could take forever, 90 years in fact. So by being part of a team, a miner gets a share of the prize which would be in the case of my machine $1.50.

With Bitcoin there is one puzzle every 10 minutes up for grabs so that's a quiz game worth almost $9m a day, and that is just for mining Bitcoin.

There are over 1,000 coins to choose from and each has a payout you can earn and turn into Bitcoin and cash, though sadly you can only mine one coin at a time.

Bitcoin is considered out of the reach of a machine like mine so I join mining pools for smaller, more obscure coins and go for the one I like the most and which pays the best.

With these mining rewards on offer there are warehouses of special computers doing this task around the world, perhaps more than 150,000 specialist machines. These can earn roughly $50 a day per machine so a factory full of them can do good business.

Even with this competition my notebook can run mining software and make me $500 a year. That is one of the beauties of the distributed nature of cryptocurrencies, they morph to try and include as many people as possible.

Becoming a Miner

So how do you get into this action?

Firstly, if you have an Apple Mac, you can skip the rest of the section about mining. Apple computers just don't have the power to play. It is really only PC users that have access to the kind of hardware necessary to mine. It sucks, but that's what comes of choosing a platform for media consumption over a computing device. Sorry, a thousand pardons to you Apple folks.

But if you have a PC you are in the game. Straight off the bat, you can get a piece of mining software by downloading for it free onto your computer and then running it.

What follows is the simplest way to proceed. It may sound scary but it is the easiest, safest way I've found.

First you need to get a 'wallet hash' from your Coinbase account. A wallet hash is the address of your account, which coins can be sent to. It's OK to give it out, your account can't be hacked with it and it is effectively an anonymous identifier. Think of a wallet hash as a PO Box number where money can be sent to you. That will be a really long set of figures like this:

1PWRRLVUTxRVB48WeapyE4zn9EVgqKf8YJ

This is one of my Bitcoin hash numbers and you can send me as many Bitcoins as you like by sending them to the above address. Please feel free, but I won't send them back, sorry.

Next, download the mining software from an outfit called Nicehash (https://www.nicehash.com/cpu-gpu-mining). I've used this and received thousands of dollars from them, so my trust level with them is high.

Then run the software and put your Bitcoin address in the window for it and press start. Then it will run and will start earning Bitcoin.

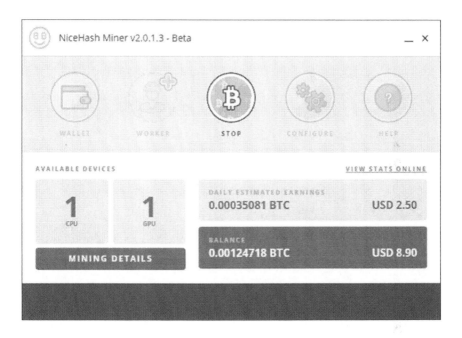

Now you are thinking, is that it? Isn't there more to it? Can it be that easy?

Yes, that's all you need to do.

But what about registering and giving details...?

Nope, you don't need to do any of that, the wallet hash was enough.

No, really? You are thinking, surely you need to pay for something or give details or email addresses?

No, you only need to put in your wallet hash, which is the Bitcoin address to send you the Bitcoin you earn (you can put mine in above if you like, if you want to send me the free money instead).

So you put your Bitcoin address in and click start. That is all there is to it. It will then check out your computer for processing power and start, using the most profitable code for your machine.

You might get $4 a day, you might get 3c a day depending on your computer. My notebook pulls in $1-$1.50 a day as it has a 1060 Nvidia graphics card in it to do the work. If your machine is weak it will earn less, if you have a burly gaming PC it could be $3-$5 a day.

This is the ground zero of mining. Download the Nicehash software, put in a Bitcoin address and click start. After about a week the resulting Bitcoins will show up in your Coinbase account.

Of course there is more to it, but that is the basics and all you need do if you want to keep it simple.

There are levels of mining because the money you make is directly connected to the power of your mining computer. Equipment has a 'hash rate' broadly defined as its puzzle processing power per second. Hash rate per second = money earned per second. The more hash rate a device has the more it costs. You also need to factor in the cost of power because if the device is power hungry, like older machines, earning will be eaten up by your electricity bill.

Broadly this is the lowdown on mining equipment.

1. Your PC.

   You can make between 10c and $4 a day with your PC depending on your central processing unit (CPU) and graphics card (GPU). You can make a few cents a day using the CPU of your computer. The CPU is the central brain of the machine but mining is so power hungry these days that to make dollars a day you need to use a graphics card like the ones made by AMD and Nvidia. The top of the line Nvidia 1080ti can make $3-$5 a day depending on the state of the market. The fancier your graphics card the more you are going to make.

2. Mining rigs with multiple graphics cards.

   A computer can't run more than one graphics card at a time. A mining rig runs as many as it can, normally six, sometimes eight or more. It has a standard PC board, a fat power supply and enough space for all the cards and as much cooling as possible. These days these rigs are a metal frame holding the whole thing together to let all that heat out. A graphics card can burn 250watts so six will give off the heat of a 1,500 watt fan heater. It's a hot noisy piece of equipment.

3. Special machines built with chips designed for mining.

   The more powerful the computer you have, the more money you make. So companies have designed special purpose-built computers to mine coins. They use application-specific integrated services (ASICs), special chips designed and built specifically to do nothing but the algo and do it fast and many times at the same time. These are the monsters that Bitcoin mines use and dwarf a GPU by factors of 10, 50, perhaps 100 times. But they are expensive and in limited supply. To buy one you have to send many thousands of dollars to China and wait for months hoping you will get your magic money machine. This is the top end of mining and it's a serious business.

Note: Electricity

Not all people pay for their electricity or pay the same rates. Mining companies move to where the cheap electricity is, be that Iceland or Mongolia, Georgia. A sneaky kid with a GPU in his bedroom computer doesn't pay for his electricity but sure would like $100 a month in extra pocket money. Someone waiting in an airport lounge gets their electricity free. Some folks live in developments where the electricity is thrown in. How many people in offices are sneakily running coin miners on their BYOD? I would venture a few.

Learning to be a Nerd

Now to go beyond just using Nicehash to take advantage of the computer you have, you must start entering the world of the nerd. You had better be a bit of a nerd to go further or be prepared to nerd up at least a little.

Building a mining rig takes a bit of skill, but it's not impossible. Kids build PCs from components all the time. You buy a case, a motherboard, a drive, install an operating system and you have a PC.

It might take several hours of watching YouTube videos, but it can be done.

For Bitcoin mining, you buy a special case called a mining rig, which is an aluminium frame, and you install a PC motherboard in it with as many graphics cards as the power supply can drive without running out of power. This is going to be between 4-6 GPUs. The best GPUs, which can make $3-$4 a day, cost $600-$800 each.

Let's say about $6,000 will get you a six-card rig and let's say it will bring in $20-$30 a day. You will probably get your money back in about nine months… with luck. Maybe prices will skyrocket and you will make more, maybe they will collapse and you will get less.

Now here is another wrinkle: the more miners there are, the more difficult it becomes to solve problems, so each card will make less over time as other people jump on the bandwagon. As such, the cards' profitability drops. At some stage it will be zero. However, it can jump if coins go up in value, so it is an ever-developing situation, with the difficulty able to drop if people give up or go to another coin to mine.

However, the ability for your rig to make money is bound to fall to zero at some stage. When is unknown. I feel there is a 100% profit in running cards for 18 months but it could be more or it could be less. The cards could produce for a longer or a shorter time.

It's a gamble. In the end you can always sell your cards back to gamers and get a fairly large chunk of your investment back.

Other Ways to Mine

If you are mining you are in the game. This is important as like all trading and investment, the profits come from knowledge and skill and there is nothing like doing to learn the business.

A mining rig can continue to use Nicehash, which selects good altcoins to mine, organises the mining, transfers the results into Bitcoin and sends that to you. I use it for my rigs, but you can also use stand-alone mining software and work out what to mine yourself and I do that too. It is a case of what you think will make you the most money and what is the most convenient.

There are several such pieces of software but I use CCMINER. It is excellent software. You download it, check out what coin you want to mine and use CCMINER and a mining pool to do it.

Now this gets a bit more elaborate.

Right now I am mining Doubloon (also known by its ticker BOAT). I have lots of good reasons and it is working out very well for me. But remember my Golden Rules, particularly 1 and 3.

CCMINER supports BOAT. So first of all I need to download the latest version of CCMINER. You can find it with a Google search. The software lives on a website called Github.com which is a kind of geek paradise.

If you are not a nerd, try not to get too disorientated by this, just grab the software and run. Then install it.

Inside you will see a lot of files that run the software for different coins. Locate the one for BOAT: it's called RUN-BOAT-YIIMP.

We will come back here later.

Getting a BOAT Wallet

Now we need to get a BOAT wallet on your PC to send the mining rewards to. You can download that from github too, but let's find out all about the coin while we do that.

To find out all you can about BOAT, use Google to locate the Doubloon (BOAT) announcement channel on: Bitcointalk.com. This site has info on most of the coins out there. It is where developers of coins launch their coins and is a central place for information.

You will find the topic on Doubloon BOAT by typing into Google:

doubloon boat coin

This takes you to the URL:

https://bitcointalk.org/index.php?topic=1776066.0. You can read about Doubloon here.

Once you have read all about it you can get set up by following these steps:

1. Scroll down that page on bitcointalk and you will see there is a link: Windows Wallet (github). Click that and go there and download the wallet. Once it is downloaded, run the wallet.

2. The first time you run the BOAT wallet, it will sync with the BOAT blockchain, the distributed ledger you will be mining. After it has synced with the BOAT blockchain, you click the receive icon and you will see your BOAT hash address.

3. Now you edit that into the CCMINER file called: RUN-BOAT-YIIMP that we found earlier. Load the file into a text editor such as Notepad (this program comes with Windows; to find it, press the Windows key then type Notepad into the search box). **Don't use Microsoft Word, it'll mess up the file!**

4. The file should look like this:

   ccminer-x64.exe -a hmq1725 -o
   stratum+tcp://yiimp.ccminer.org:3747 -u **your-BOAT-HASH-here** -p c=BOAT,d=128,stats pause

   Replace the part that says **your-BOAT-HASH-here** with your BOAT hash address and save the file.

5. Then you run CCMINER by clicking on the newly edited file RUN-BOAT-YIIMP.

All the messages running down the screen mean you are mining on the yiimp.ccminer.org mining pool and in an hour or two coins will start showing up in your wallet.

If you go to http://yiimp.ccminer.org you can see the pool at work and if you enter your hash into the site on the wallet page you will see how you are getting on.

Your hash is both your ID and password; everyone can see it but no one can access your coins or know who owns them. It is one of the cool features of cryptocurrencies.

> **Note: An illustration of the dangers**
> While I've been writing this short book, the YIIMP pool and all the other pools using the codebase were hacked. Coins were stolen, although small amounts in comparison to many hacks. Happily, coins are paid out every hour by such pools, so I didn't lose anything worth mentioning. The developers jumped in and fixed the security hole and the pools came back up in the following days, bruised but not broken. However, it demonstrates once again that you cannot be too paranoid. I am using them again because, while I don't trust the internet, I trust the pool developers.

Now http://yiimp.ccminer.org is not the only pool out there, there are many, but I use it as it is run by the developers of CCMINER.

Another is http://www.zpool.ca/.

There are many coins and many ways to mine them and I feel it's a profitable road to travel along. It is also a key part of understanding cryptocurrency and what makes it tick. In this way it is a training that pays.

Once you have mastered a program like CCMINER you can mine lots of different coins. You can chase the most profitable ones of the day by using sites like Coinwarz.com and Whattomine.com. These sites let you specify your equipment and suggest the profit you can make in a day. It's fun and frankly when money just appears in your Coinbase account it's a little magical.

There are downsides. Mining rigs generate a lot of heat and a fair amount of noise from cooling fans. Four GPUs running is like having a 1K fan heater on in the room. Make sure you have the cheapest electricity plan you can get because running a rig does cost money, the same way as running a fan heater or an air-conditioning unit does. If you like your computer to run quietly then mining is not for you.

Even so, the money rolls in and you can use the profit calculators above to work out if it is worth your while.

Remember in the end, if you are fed up with your noisy hot mining rig, you can always sell the graphics cards on eBay and get a good chunk of your outlay back.

So let us say it takes 18 months to make a fat profit, let's imagine you have doubled your money, at which stage the GPU cards can't mine enough to pay for their keep. Every penny you get back selling the cards is pure profit and you may get as much as half your money back or even more if coin prices have gone yet higher.

Of course, you might reinvest that in ASIC miners or the latest GPUs because there will still be coins that will need miners and will pay a fat return for anyone prepared to offer that service.

ASIC Miners

Finally, there are specialist ASIC miners. These machines are currently made in China, designed specifically to mine coins. They have dozens, perhaps hundreds, of special chips in them that do nothing but the puzzle-solving task. They can cost as much as $10,000 each and you have to pay up front months in advance to mystery companies in China and hope and pray you will get your machine in a few months' time.

Why take the risk?

Because the machine will pay for itself in 90 days and earn $50-$300 a day for one to three years. That's $40,000 to $120,000 a year... maybe.

The 'maybe' is, the market might crash, which could make it difficult to get your money back. If the mystery company in China never delivers, you are scuppered. If the machine breaks down or never works, what then? These are the risks and are weighed against potentially huge returns.

Who would take the risk?

The answer is, these machines sell out in hours. They sell out faster than tickets for a Pink Floyd comeback tour. With that kind of possible profit people will take the risk and they have paid off time and again.

Why do the companies sell their machines like this?

The answer would appear to be that they fund their production run of new equipment for their mining operations with your money from the initial sale and keep 50%-70% of the production for their own mines. They sell machines to a few hungry outsiders, which gives them a risk-free production ride where they make money and get the bulk of the machines with which they make $40,000 to $120,000 a year per machine.

It's a no-risk, no-lose trade.

The outside purchasers are promoters of the coins they mine which helps bolster the very price of the coins they are mining.

Selling some of a production run produces a virtuous circle. It also fulfils the old maxim of how to make money in a gold rush: "to make a fortune in a gold rush, sell picks and shovels."

These are very clever people making very clever equipment and a lot of money.

If you want to go big in mining you either make GPU rigs or bet on ASIC mining equipment. It feels pretty dicey, but when the coins show up and you can turn them into dollars or euros it suddenly feels a lot less insane.

We are accustomed to our usual state of financial affairs, but they are hardly less strange and abstract than the way cryptocurrency works. Our wealth has been held on spinning disks of rust dependant on electricity from far away for years now, but familiarity makes it seem normal. It is the novelty of cryptocurrency that makes it seem surreal.

Summary

Computers do accounting chores and are paid to do so if they can solve puzzles. These puzzles require a lot of computing power provided by a hierarchy of devices. You can make pennies mining with your PC, dollars with a gaming computer, $30 upwards with a mining rig and $50+ with the right ASIC miner.

The costs are from nothing to a lot, say $10,000 for a single ASIC device. You can check the figures online and gauge if you can afford to play.

Remember, if you don't fancy mining you can always just buy coins.

Chapter 8: The Technical Stuff

So you wanted to get 'into' cryptocoins fast and you wanted to know how. The technical stuff is not so interesting. But it is important to cover because cryptocurrency is incredibly complex and hard to understand. To trade and invest successfully you have to dig into this uber-nerdy stuff because otherwise you will just be gambling. There is nothing wrong with gambling but it is understood that gamblers lose and we don't want to do that.

Now while you wait for various websites to open your accounts, here is some basic information to simply explain what the devil these things are.

What is a Bitcoin or an Altcoin or a Cryptocurrency?

First of all, let's treat **BITCOIN** as the basic cryptocurrency. It's the king of cryptocurrencies, it's the first, it's the generic, so let's talk about Bitcoin. All other coins are a permutation on the Bitcoin story so Bitcoin is the specimen case.

Like your money in your bank or perhaps your overdraft, a Bitcoin is an entry in a book of records called a ledger. This ledger entry is held on a computer and once upon a time would have been penned on the page of a book. When you query the ledger it gives up a record and a balance saying how much you have. For the Bitcoin Ledger it might be:

You have 1.153567 BTC

A fraction of a Bitcoin is called a **SATOSHI**. There are 100 million satoshi fractions to one whole Bitcoin.

The ledger is called a **BLOCKCHAIN**, which can be imagined as a linked series of pages where records are kept. The blockchain is kept on many computers spread around the internet on servers. Anyone can have a copy of it and can host it and can keep the ledger.

Using encryption, which keeps most of the information secret, the blockchain can be held anywhere by anyone and manipulated from anywhere.

This apparently crazy system is moderated by a process where people holding a copy of the blockchain and people maintaining the ledger itself enforce and keep the blockchain uncorrupted, up-to-date and secure.

Blockchain technology is a **PLATFORM**, just like a computer operating system, or a browser. It can enable more than just a cryptocurrency, but this is where the application of blockchain has taken off first.

So when you hear about blockchain as a platform for amazing new things, it is not necessarily about Bitcoin and other cryptocurrencies, it could be about lots of other uses where a distributed, open but secure database would be tremendously useful, for example contracts or any registry of documents.

How a blockchain works exactly is to dive down a very deep rabbit hole, so we are not going to, but it's clever and very complex and is a technical breakthrough set to bring a lot of changes to our lives.

People who maintain and update records on the blockchain are called **MINERS**. Anyone can be a miner, you don't need permission. Miners' servers do this administration task and are given a

REWARD by the system in new coins, which the system writes to the blockchain into the miner's Bitcoin account. Currently this is 12 Bitcoins per block reward and at the recent $5,000 a coin you can see that is a lot of money. It is enough money for people to build factories full of machines to mine Bitcoin and crack their proof of work (POW) puzzles.

A Bitcoin account is called a **HASH** and is stored on the blockchain. The hash is an address made up of nonsense characters and when this address is searched for in the blockchain, it will return the balance held by it. These hash addresses are like account codes you have at your bank, except they are much longer. Here is one of mine:

178iyJuekJfBgDGRPQT92USbYiXutCptXF

The blockchain is easy to build but to limit the issue of new coins and make the blockchain a limited and valuable resource, a puzzle is set to the miners to solve before they can make new entries into the blockchain and get their reward.

If they solve this puzzle that creates the next record in the blockchain, which is called a **BLOCK**. The block will hold a number of transaction records from Bitcoin transactions that have been done recently and need to be made official amongst all the blockchain copies on the Bitcoin network.

Miners on the network will confirm their agreement that this new block is good and when enough have given the OK to other servers on the network, the funds in the transactions, including the reward to the miner, are cleared.

The puzzle set to the miners is via an **ALGO**; for Bitcoin it is the SHA256 algo. This is a cryptographic puzzle and it is entwined into how the whole system works to make the ledger secure.

As more and more miners throw more and more computing power at solving the puzzles needed to earn Bitcoins by mining, thereby updating and maintaining the blockchain, so the algo makes harder puzzles to keep the rewards coming at an even rate. This is the monetary policy of the coin and it affects its value by regulating supply and demand.

In due course the number of coins in a reward is halved and at some point there will be no more rewards for the miners and new coins will cease to be made. There is a **MAXIMUM COIN CAP** and this is 21 million for Bitcoin.

However, there is still money to be made by the miners. Every transaction has a **FEE** attached. In Bitcoin this is currently $3-5 a go, but for small less heavyweight coins it can be tiny fractions of a US cent. The Bitcoin system lets the miners decide which transactions to register into a block and therefore prioritise transactions in terms of how important the transacting party thinks his transaction is.

When a miner cracks a puzzle he gets the fees of the transaction, which can amount to thousands of dollars of Bitcoin.

Bitcoin rewards are currently the main driver of the system but fees are increasingly important and will in years to come take over from the rewards for mining a block.

Bitcoins are stored in **WALLETS**. This isn't what it sounds like; really the term is incorrect because the wallets are actually keys to the record in the blockchain of your Bitcoins. These keys let you move your coins and thereby pay people or transfer your coins to other addresses. The wallet on your computer or mobile doesn't hold the Bitcoins, it holds the keys to transacting them on the blockchain. A PC/Mobile wallet is like the online bank account you hold, in as much as the money is not on your computer, it is held in a database far away and is viewed and dealt with via software on your computer.

Altcoins

So that's how Bitcoins work. But what about all these **ALTCOINS**, these other cryptocurrencies?

There are a plethora of other coins but none as big or successful as Bitcoin. Where are they coming from?

Bitcoin is an open source software project, so you could get the source code for Bitcoin from the internet, recompile it with a new name and create a new start block of a new blockchain, the so called **GENESIS BLOCK**, and you would have your own coin, let us call it Spinachcoin.

This is a Bitcoin **FORK**. This fork is like a fork in the road, not a fork in the spaghetti. When you read about forks and forking, it is about messing with an existing coin's codebase to create changes in the way it works or make a brand new coin. If you forked Spinachcoin you might call the new coin Cabbagecoin and it may or may not do something new and useful depending on how much effort you put into the fork.

Anyone can fork Bitcoin or other coins, as much as they like. It is not easy, but school kids have done it. Getting people to care is a much harder thing and a Spinachcoin fork of Bitcoin would win no believers and would sit on a server somewhere totally ignored and worthless. A coin from a fork cannot interact with the original because miners would have to choose to do so and they won't.

If for some magical reason all the miners wanted to mine Spinachcoin and stop mining Bitcoin, it would be a different matter, but people do not behave like that. Spinachcoin is not going to take off as a simple fork of Bitcoin.

Meanwhile, the Bitcoin system can be forked in infinite ways. You could change the reward, the time between blocks being made, the size of blocks, the algo used to make the puzzle and tweak it in many permutations and you would end up with a valid coin. You could give it special functionality like Ethereum – the possibilities are endless.

Spinachcoin would be born and could take off, if it had good reason to. Yet it wouldn't hurt Bitcoin because that coin would carry on in its own ecosystem adding value doing what it always did.

Meanwhile you could create a mining pool for Spinachcoin, get it listed on a cryptocurrency exchange, promote it, get a popstar to use it, make an ICO and try to make it the next big thing. People are doing this and some have succeeded. This is where altcoins come from.

What we are trying to do is pick the winners from this process and we do that by evaluating the qualities of new and existing coins.

Let us imagine that Spinachcoin has a dazzling team behind it. Then we understand it makes your iPhone battery last twice as long if you install the wallet on your mobile (this is a joke example so don't go looking for the Spinachcoin ICO), then we see it is a low satoshi coin with a low market cap currently, sowe would definitely want to load up on Spinachcoin to lock away its long-term upside.

New coins like this are appearing regularly and some will be hugely successful. They will likely share a family tree with Bitcoin and be forks of forks.

Nothing is simple in the world of cryptocurrencies.

Reviews

"Clem re-skins classic trading strategies for the cryptocurrency age. A new game is in town. A must-read for everyone who wants to have their finger on the pulse and see how money is being made now." *Alpesh Patel*

"A great guide to trading a crazy market." *Robbie Burns*

"This is an invaluable 'how to' for anyone looking to enter into the exciting world of cyrptocurrencies trading. It's a truly warts and all guide explaining and demonstrating numerous techniques and ideas for actually making money in this high risk, high reward environment." *NEWSBTC.com*

"When you're in the Wild West you need to know who sells the best guns and who the good guys are. You also need a good horse. Clem Chambers' handy and timely book is all of those things when it comes to the tools of the trade for would-be crypto traders.

In a red-hot market that won't last forever, and with fortunes to be made by those who know their way around the canyons and plains, knowing how to capture the spread, arbitrage exchanges and deploy effective criteria to judge which coins will fly and which will die, this is an essential handbook for those seeking to profit from the future of money.

Chambers' killer insight is invaluable: in the analogue world the brokers and exchanges make the market by buying low and selling high; in cryptoland everyone can be their own broker. We can all see the order book and 'capture the spread', it just takes practice and experience. You also learn how to mine digital gold 'in them there hills' – actually on your laptop, which is a great way to earn while you do the hands-on learning about how cryptocurrencies works." *Gary McFarlane, cryptocurrency writer at Money Observer*

About The Author

Clem Chambers is a freelance journalist covering global finance, economics and investing.

He is CEO of ADVFN, a global stocks and shares information website, author of the Amazon No.1 Bestseller *101 Ways to Pick Stock Market Winners* and a Forbes and IET (Institute of Engineering and Technology) columnist. He has been nominated for PPA business columnist of the year 2016 and 2017 for his writing in the latter. In June 2017 he won silver in the Tabbie Awards for his Money and Markets column in E&T Magazine.

A broadcast and print media regular, Chambers is a familiar face and frequent guest presenter on CNBC and CNBC Europe. He has been a market commentator and guest on the BBC, Fox News, CNBC Arabia, Newsnight, Al Jazeera, CNN, SKY News, TF1, Canada's Business News Network and numerous US radio stations.

Clem has written investment columns for Wired Magazine, Business Mirror, Inversionista, Index Trader, Traders, Gulf News, YTE, RiskAFRICA and the Scotsman and has been a commentator for The Daily Mail, The Daily Telegraph, The Guardian, The Independent and The Daily Express.

Clem has written several books for ADVFN Books, including **101 Ways To Pick Stock Market Winners, A Beginner's Guide to Value Investing, The Death of Wealth** and **Letters to my Broker**.

In the last few years he has become a successful financial thriller writer, authoring **The Twain Maxim, The Armageddon Trade, Kusanagi, The First Horseman** and **The Shrine**. He has also written techno-thrillers set during the dawn of the internet, **Dial Up for Murder** and **Log On for Crime**.

Clem also writes for the ADVFN newspaper and has two premium newsletters: Diary of a Contrarian Investor and Building an Income Portfolio. He also co-writes a premium newsletter with Brokerman Dan: Jekyll & Hyde Share Tips.

This is Clem's seventh book for ADVFN Books. Turn over for details of his other books

Also by Clem Chambers

ADVFN Guide: 101 Ways to Pick Stock Market Winners

101 tips to help day traders, investors and stock pickers to focus on what characterises a potentially successful stock. Personally researched by Clem Chambers, one of the world's leading authorities on market performance. Incisive, brutally honest and occasionally very funny, *101 Ways to Pick Stock Market Winners* is an invaluable manual for anyone wanting to make money out of the markets.

Available for the Kindle.

ADVFN Guide: The Beginner's Guide to Value Investing

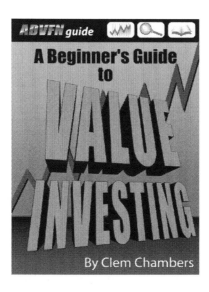

The stock market is not only for rich people, or those intent on gambling. 'Value Investing' is how Warren Buffet became the richest man in the world. A method of investing in the stock market without taking crazy risks, 'Value Investing' will help you build your fortune, no matter the economic climate. Perfect for novice investors, the book clearly outlines how to choose the best stocks and how – thanks to the Internet. It is the perfect way to ensure you 'get rich slow' with minimal stress.

Available in paperback and for the Kindle.

The Game in Wall Street

by Hoyle and Clem Chambers

As the new century dawned, Wall Street was a game and the stock market was fixed. Ordinary investors were fleeced by big institutions that manipulated the markets to their own advantage and they had no comeback.

The Game in Wall Street shows the ways that the titans of rampant capitalism operated to make money from any source they could control. Their accumulated funds gave the titans enormous power over the market and allowed them to ensure they won the game.

Traders joining the game without knowing the rules are on a road to ruin. It's like gambling without knowing the rules and with no idea of the odds.

The Game in Wall Street sets out in detail exactly how this market manipulation works and shows how to ride the price movements and make a profit.

And guess what? The rules of the game haven't changed since the book was first published in 1898. You can apply the same strategies in your own investing and avoid losing your shirt by gambling against the professionals.

Illustrated with the very first stock charts ever published, the book contains a new preface and a conclusion by stock market guru Clem Chambers which put the text in the context of how Wall Street operates today.

Available in paperback and for the Kindle.

The Death of Wealth

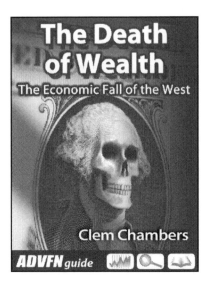

Question: what is the next economic game changer?
Answer: The Death of Wealth.

Market guru Clem Chambers dissects the global economy and the state of the financial markets and lays out the evidence for the death of wealth.

The Death of Wealth flags up the milestones on the route towards impending financial disaster. From the first tentative signs of recovery in the UK and US stock markets at the start of 2012, to the temporary drawing back from the edge of the Fiscal Cliff at the end, the book chronicles the trials and tribulations of the markets throughout the year.

Collecting together articles and essays throughout the last twelve months along with extensive new analysis for 2013, *The Death of Wealth* allows us to look at these tumultuous events collectively and draw a strong conclusion about what the future holds.

2012 started with the US economy showing signs of recovery, and European financial markets recovering some of the ground lost during the euro crisis. It ended with Obama's re-election and the deal that delayed the plunge off the fiscal cliff by a few months.

In between, the eurozone crisis continued, but none of the affected countries actually left the eurozone; quantitative easing tried to turn things around with the consequences of these 'unorthodox' actions yet unknown; and the equity markets after the mid-year correction became strongly bullish.

The Death of Wealth takes you through the events of 2012 month by month, with charts showing the movements of the FTSE 100, the NASDAQ COMPX and the SSE COMPX throughout the year.

With an introduction by renowned market commentator and stock tipster Tom Winnifrith and a summary by trading technical analyst Zak Mir, this collection chronicles the rocky road trip the financial systems of the world have been on and predicts the ultimate destination: the death of wealth as we know it.

Available in paperback and for the Kindle.

ADVFN'S Be Rich

How to make 25% a year investing sensibly in shares – a real time demonstration

Investing is easy – when you know what you are doing. Otherwise, it's hard, and risky. For a new investor, "playing" the stock market can be a huge and often costly learning curve. How to climb it? This book takes you up that mountain.

Over the course of a year, Clem Chambers built a contrarian value investing portfolio **from scratch** and chronicled his investing choices, sharing them with subscribers to his newsletter. The portfolios earned him a 25% return.

Now you can benefit from that expertise, see the process and experience the ride – the whole process laid bare.

Clem explains the strategies he uses as he builds the portfolio, sharing the highs and the lows: sometimes the market makes him look like a fool, sometimes a genius, but over the year the market pays out because it is no one decision or one market trend that makes for successful investing but a consistent approach that delivers profits.

Be Rich will show you the way.

Available in paperback and for the Kindle.

Letters to My Broker

P.S. What do you think of the Market?

"Why is it the minute I sell my stocks, no matter which they are, right away they go up?"

Meet Joe, a rich but hapless investor who makes every mistake possible. Just when you think he's learnt something, he finds a new way to lose money.

Populated by rogues, hucksters and fools *Letters to my Broker* is the classic comedy of errors revived for a new generation that teaches you the rules to trading the stock market haven't changed in the 94 years since its original publication.

"I want some advice. Not that I'll follow it."

Aided by the acerbic commentary of No. 1 bestselling author and ADVFN CEO Clem Chambers, *Letters to my Broker* tells you where

Joe's going wrong, what you should do to keep your shirt and how to avoid his hilarious errors.

Stock market tips so old they're new: Read *Letters to my Broker* and trade like it's 1919.

Available in paperback and for the Kindle.

For more information go to the ADVFN Books website at www.advfnbooks.com.

Printed in Great Britain
by Amazon